# My Very Own

# THANKSGIVING

## A Book of Cooking and Crafts

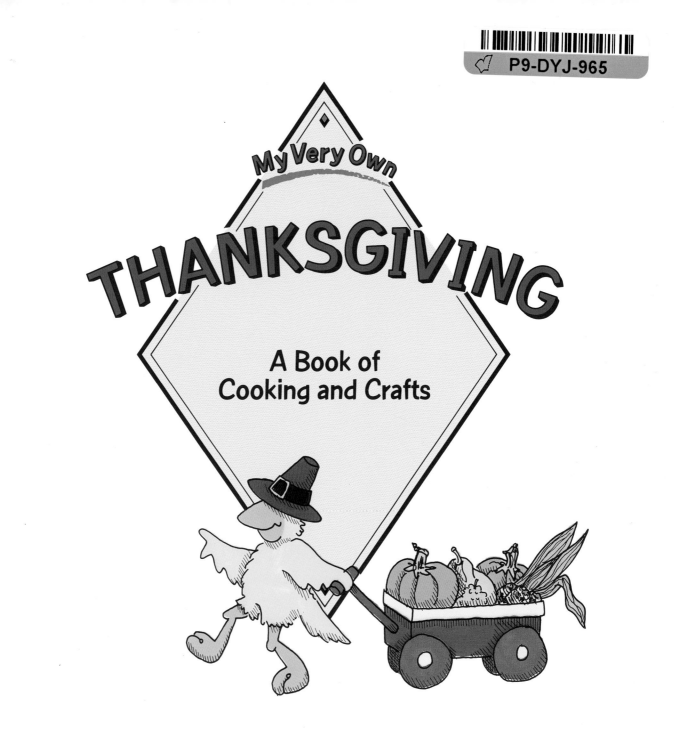

# My Very Own

# THANKSGIVING

## A Book of
## Cooking and Crafts

by Robin West

photographs by Robert L. and Diane Wolfe
illustrations by Susan Slattery Burke

Carolrhoda Books, Inc./Minneapolis

*To Mom and Dad*

Library of Congress Cataloging-in-Publication Data

West, Robin.
    My very own Thanksgiving : a book of cooking and
crafts / by Robin West ; photographs by Robert L. and
Diane Wolfe ; illustrations by Susan Slattery Burke.
    p.   cm. — (My very own holiday books)
    Includes index.
    Summary: A collection of Thanksgiving recipes and
crafts, accompanied by information about the holiday.
    ISBN 0-87614-723-6
    1. Thanksgiving cookery — Juvenile literature.
2. Thanksgiving decorations — Juvenile literature.
3. Handicraft — Juvenile literature.  [1. Thanksgiving
cookery.  2. Thanksgiving decorations.  3. Cookery,
American.  4. Handicraft.]  I. Wolfe, Robert L.  II. Wolfe,
Diane.  III. Burke, Susan Slattery, ill.  IV. Title.  V. Series:
West, Robin. My very own holiday books.
TX739.2.T45W47 1993
641.5'68—dc20                              92-33234
                                                          CIP
                                                          AC

Manufactured in the United States of America

1   2   3   4   5   6   98   97   96   95   94   93

# Contents

My Very Own THANKSGIVING

# Thanksgiving Greetings

It happens every year, as autumn is ending and winter draws near. Mothers and fathers and brothers and sisters, aunts and uncles and grandmas and grandpas all gather together, dressed in their holiday best. Tempting foods simmer on the stove, filling the air with mouth-watering smells. It's a terrible time to be a turkey but a great time to be a kid. It's Thanksgiving!

You don't have to wait for Thanksgiving Day for the holiday fun to begin. Getting ready for Thanksgiving can be almost as much fun as the holiday itself. Put together some paper dolls to greet holiday guests, or make a festive centerpiece to brighten your table. You might even try having a party and making the food yourself (with a little help from an adult friend). The possibilities are endless, so you'd better get started because Thanksgiving will be here before you know it!

# Make It Your Very Own:
## How to Use This Book

### RECIPES

The recipes in this book are divided into five menus, but you don't have to make a whole meal.
If you are a new cook, start slowly. Choose a recipe that sounds good to you and try it out. You might need lots of help to begin with, but be patient. The more you practice, the better you'll be.

*Here are some of the easier recipes to get you started:*

Sparkling Cider
Festive Orange Salad
Halftime Ham Nibbles
Seaworthy Raisin Rafts

Once you know what you're doing, it's time to make a whole meal. Try one of the menus, or put together your own combination.

*Here are some things to consider when planning a menu:*

*Nutrition:* Balance your menu by choosing something from each of the four food groups: breads, dairy products, fruits and vegetables, and meat and other proteins. You can fill out your menu with foods that don't need recipes, such as bread, fresh fruits, milk, cheese, and raw vegetables.

*Variety:* Include different tastes and textures in your meal. If one food is soft and creamy, serve it with something crunchy. Salty foods taste good when served with something sweet. Try to include a variety of colors so the food is as pretty to look at as it is good to eat.

*Theme:* Each of the menus in this

book has a theme, just to make it more fun. Try to think up a theme of your own, and choose recipes that go with it. How about a menu of foods that can be eaten with your fingers? Why not serve a fall colors meal, including bright orange Savory Cheese Soup and rich brown Chilly Chocolate Pumpkin Pie? Or forget about planning a meal, and make a variety of desserts instead. Anything is possible!

Be sure to share your masterpiece with someone else. Whether you make one dish or an entire meal, half the fun of cooking is watching someone else enjoy the food.

## CRAFTS

Like the recipes, all of the crafts in this book are easy to make, but some are easier than others. If you haven't tried making crafts before, start with something easy, like some It's a Party! Invitations or a Shipshape Placemat. As you gain confidence, put together some Here Come the Turkeys Napkin Rings or a Falling Leaves Centerpiece. Once you've tackled these crafts, you're ready to make Hand-in-Hand Paper Dolls.

Don't be afraid to use your imagination when decorating your crafts. Use markers, colored construction paper, scraps of fabric, or even glitter to give your craft a personal touch.

# Cooking Smart

*Whether you are a new or experienced cook, these cooking tips can help you avoid a kitchen disaster.*

### BEFORE YOU COOK

• Get yourself ready. If you have long hair, tie it back to keep it out of the food, away from flames, and out of your way. Roll up your sleeves, and put on an apron. And be sure to wash your hands well with soap.

• Read through the entire recipe and assemble all of the ingredients. It's no fun to find out halfway through a recipe that you're out of eggs.

• Go through the recipe with an adult helper and decide which steps you can perform yourself and which you'll need help with.

### WHILE YOU COOK

• Raw meat and raw eggs can contain dangerous bacteria. After handling these raw foods, wash your hands and any utensils or cutting boards you've used. Never put cooked meat on an unwashed plate that has held raw meat. Any dough that contains raw eggs isn't safe to eat until it's cooked.

• Keep cold foods in the refrigerator until you need them.

• Wash fruits and vegetables thoroughly before using them.

• Turn pot handles to the back of the stove so the pots won't be knocked off by accident. When you are taking the lid off a hot pan, always keep the opening away from your face so the steam won't burn you.

• Use a pot holder when handling hot pans. Be sure the pot holder is dry before you use it. The heat from the pan will come right through a wet pot holder.

- Always turn off the stove or oven as soon as you're done with it.
- Be careful with foods when they come out of the microwave. Although the food may seem to be cool to the touch, microwaving can produce hot spots. When you're heating a liquid in the microwave, stir it often to distribute the heat evenly.
- Only use microwave-safe dishes in the microwave. Never put anything metal in the microwave.
- Don't cut up food in your hand. Use a cutting board.
- Carry knives point down.
- Be careful when opening cans. The edges of the lids are very sharp.
- Don't save the mess for the end. Try to clean up as you go along.

## AFTER YOU COOK

- Once you've finished cooking, be sure to store your creation in the refrigerator if it contains any ingredients that might spoil.
- Be a courteous cook: clean up your mess. Leave the kitchen looking as clean as (or cleaner than) you found it.

## SOME CRAFTY TIPS

Assembling a craft is a lot like cooking, and many of the same tips apply. Read the instructions and gather your supplies before you start. Play it safe with your supplies, especially scissors, and be sure to get an adult friend to help you when you need it. Put down newspapers to protect your work surface. And, of course, be sure to clean up your mess when you're done.

# Harvest Feast

Heapin' Helpin' Chicken

▼

Squanto's Squash

▼

Basket o' Biscuits

▼

Chilly Chocolate
Pumpkin Pie

▼

*Falling Leaves
Centerpiece*

# Heapin' Helpin' Chicken

**YOU WILL NEED:**

1 6-ounce package wild and white rice mix, uncooked

1 chicken, cut into pieces

1 $10\frac{3}{4}$-ounce can cream of mushroom soup

1 4-ounce can sliced mushrooms, drained

2 cups water

1 Preheat oven to 375°.

2 In a 9- by 13-inch baking pan, combine rice mix with packaged seasoning.

3 Place chicken pieces on rice.

4 In a small bowl, combine soup and mushrooms. Add water little by little, stirring after each addition. Pour soup mixture over chicken.

5 Cover pan with foil and bake for 1 hour.

6 Remove foil and bake for another 30 minutes.

Serves 6

# Squanto's Squash

YOU WILL NEED:

1½ to 2 pounds acorn squash, peeled and cut into bite-size pieces (about 7 cups)

1 10¾-ounce can cream of chicken soup

1 medium carrot, peeled and grated

1 small onion, peeled and grated

¾ cup sour cream

dash pepper

⅓ cup butter or margarine, melted

1½ cups packaged herb stuffing mix

1. Preheat oven to 350°.

2. Place squash in a large kettle and cover with water. Cook over high heat, uncovered, until water comes to a boil. Remove from heat and drain squash in a colander.

3. In a large bowl, combine soup, carrot, onion, sour cream, and pepper. Stir well. Add squash and toss gently to coat with soup mixture.

4. Pour into large casserole dish.

5. In a small bowl, combine butter and stuffing mix and stir.

6. Sprinkle stuffing mixture on top of squash.

7. Bake for 45 minutes or until golden brown and bubbly.

**Serves 6**

# The First Thanksgiving

In 1620, a group of 102 Pilgrims landed on the coast of North America and established Plymouth Colony. Life in their new home was very hard. Almost half of the Pilgrims died that first winter. The remaining people probably would have died the following year if not for the help of a Native American man named Squanto.

Squanto was born into the Patuxet tribe. When he was younger, he had been captured by English fishermen and taken to Europe to be sold as a slave. Five years later, he returned home to find that most of the Patuxets had died from disease. So Squanto joined the Wampanoag tribe.

Squanto, was a good friend to the Pilgrims. He helped them build warm, sturdy homes. He taught them how to hunt and how to farm. Squanto and the Pilgrims worked hard and were rewarded with a good crop of corn in the fall.

The Pilgrims decided to give thanks for their good fortune with a celebration. They had Squanto invite some of the Wampanoag people to their feast. There was plenty of food for everyone. While they didn't have stuffing or pumpkin pie, they did have turkey. They probably also ate boiled pumpkin and cranberries sweetened with honey, along with other foods like fish and corn bread. This celebration, which lasted for three days, will always be remembered as the first Thanksgiving.

# Basket o' Biscuits

1 cup packaged biscuit mix

½ cup sour cream

¼ cup butter or margarine, softened

1. Preheat oven to 450°. Grease a muffin tin.

2. In a medium bowl, combine all ingredients and stir until sour cream and butter are combined. The dough will be lumpy.

3. Drop spoonfuls of dough into muffin tin.

4. Bake for 10 to 12 minutes or until biscuits are golden brown.

**Makes 9 to 12 biscuits**

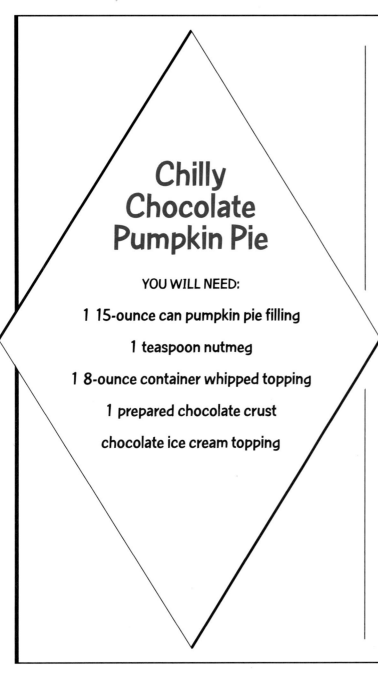

# Chilly Chocolate Pumpkin Pie

YOU WILL NEED:

1 15-ounce can pumpkin pie filling

1 teaspoon nutmeg

1 8-ounce container whipped topping

1 prepared chocolate crust

chocolate ice cream topping

1 In a medium bowl, combine pumpkin pie filling and nutmeg and stir well.

2 Fold in whipped topping.

3 Pour mixture into pie crust and smooth with a spoon.

4 With a spoon, drizzle chocolate topping over pie.

5 Freeze for at least 4 hours. Remove from freezer 20 to 30 minutes before serving.

Serves 6

# Falling Leaves Centerpiece

**YOU WILL NEED:**

5 large leaves
(different shapes and sizes)

construction paper
(red, yellow, light brown, and dark brown)

pencil

scissors

1 toilet paper tube

white liquid glue

masking tape

tracing paper

## THE LEAVES:

**1** Place a leaf on construction paper and trace around it. Repeat with remaining four leaves, using different colors of construction paper. Cut out leaves.

**2** Cut toilet paper tube in half lengthwise. Cut each half into 1-inch curved strips.

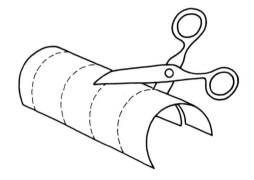

**3** Glue one or two of the curved strips to the back of each construction paper leaf to give it a curved surface. Secure the glued strips with tape. (Use the glue sparingly so the tape will stick.)

You can cover the curved strips with construction paper if you like.

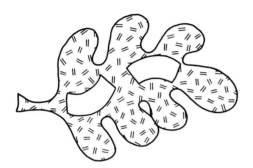

4 Group your leaves in an interesting arrangement and glue them together on the underside. Secure the leaves with tape.

### THE ACORNS:

1 Place tracing paper on top of figure A on page 21 and trace around it. Cut out tracing paper pattern. Place pattern on light brown construction paper and trace around it. Move pattern and trace around it again. Repeat one more time to make three acorns. Cut them out.

2 Place tracing paper on top of figure B on page 21 and trace around it. Cut out tracing paper pattern. Place pattern on dark brown construction paper and trace around it. Move pattern and trace around it again. Repeat one more time to make three acorn caps. Cut them out.

3 Glue caps to tops of acorns.

4 Position acorns decoratively on leaves and glue them in place.

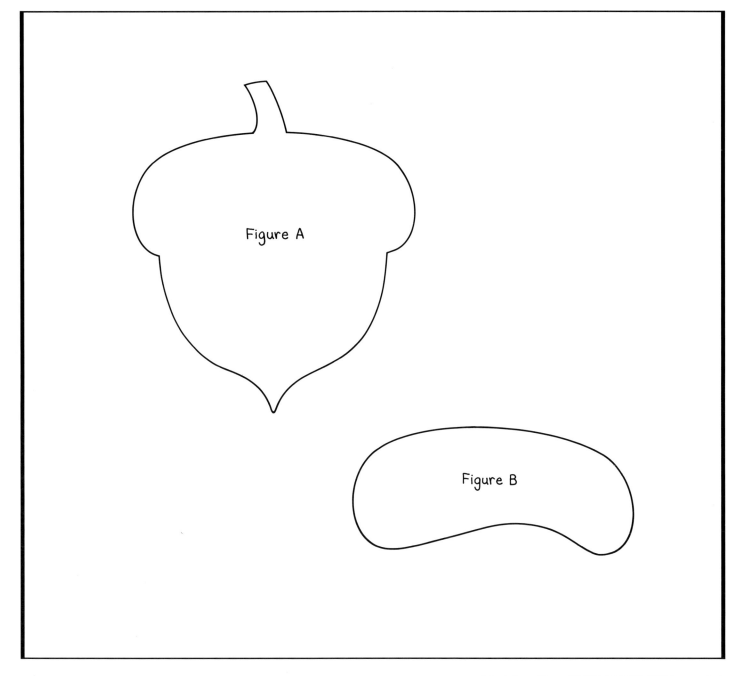

Figure A

Figure B

# Take Pity on the Turkey

Savory Cheese Soup

▼

Eat Your Veggies Pizza

▼

Sparkling Cider

▼

Just Peachy

▼

*Here Come the Turkeys Napkin Rings*

# Savory Cheese Soup

**YOU WILL NEED:**

2 tablespoons butter or margarine

1 medium onion, peeled and minced

1 clove garlic, peeled and minced

2 tablespoons cornstarch

3 cups chicken broth or vegetable broth

2 medium carrots, peeled and shredded

3 cups shredded American cheese

1 cup water

1. Melt butter in a large saucepan.

2. Add onion and garlic and cook over medium heat until onion is transparent.

3. Stir in cornstarch.

4. Add 1 cup chicken broth little by little, stirring after each addition.

5. Add carrots and stir.

6. Add cheese little by little, stirring well after each addition. Continue to stir until cheese is melted.

7. Stir in remaining 2 cups chicken broth and 1 cup water.

8. Reduce heat to low and simmer for 30 minutes.

Serves 4

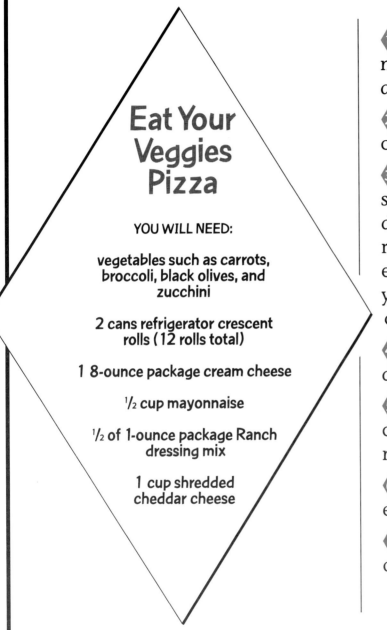

# Eat Your Veggies Pizza

**YOU WILL NEED:**

vegetables such as carrots, broccoli, black olives, and zucchini

2 cans refrigerator crescent rolls (12 rolls total)

1 8-ounce package cream cheese

½ cup mayonnaise

½ of 1-ounce package Ranch dressing mix

1 cup shredded cheddar cheese

1 Clean vegetables and peel if necessary. Cut into bite-size pieces and set aside.

2 Preheat oven to temperature called for on crescent roll package.

3 Separate dough into triangular sections. Arrange triangles of dough side by side in a circle on a round 14-inch pizza pan. Press the edges of the dough together with your fingers to make one large circle of dough.

4 Bake according to package directions.

5 In a small bowl, combine cream cheese, mayonnaise, and dressing mix and stir well.

6 Spread cream cheese mixture evenly over the cooled crust.

7 Arrange vegetables attractively on crust. Sprinkle with cheese.

**Serves 6 to 8**

# Sparkling Cider

**YOU WILL NEED:**

3½ to 4 cups cranberry juice

3 cups chilled apple cider

2 cups chilled sparkling water

½ cup fresh lemon juice

1 orange, thinly sliced

1 lemon, thinly sliced

1 lime, thinly sliced

❶ Pour cranberry juice into two ice cube trays.

❷ Freeze for 4 to 6 hours, until set.

❸ Remove cranberry cubes from ice cube trays, and place cubes in a large pitcher or punch bowl.

❹ Add cider, sparkling water, and lemon juice and stir to combine.

❺ Add orange, lemon, and lime slices and serve.

**Serves 4 to 6**

## Just Peachy

**YOU WILL NEED:**

1 10-ounce container frozen raspberries

2 tablespoons sugar

4 canned peach halves

4 scoops vanilla ice cream

**1** In a blender, blend raspberries and sugar until smooth.

**2** Place a peach half rounded-side-up on a plate. Top with a scoop of ice cream. Spoon raspberry sauce over ice cream.

**Serves 4**

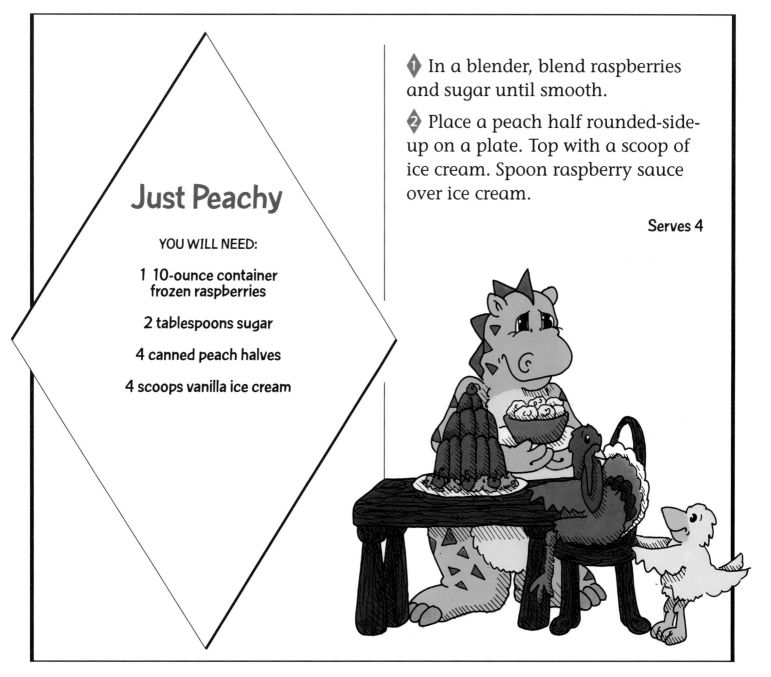

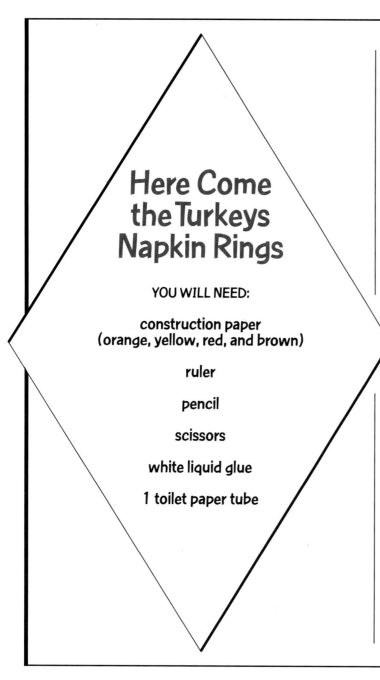

# Here Come the Turkeys Napkin Rings

**YOU WILL NEED:**

construction paper
(orange, yellow, red, and brown)

ruler

pencil

scissors

white liquid glue

1 toilet paper tube

## THE TAIL:

❶ On orange construction paper, draw two ¼- by 5-inch rectangles and two ¼- by 3-inch rectangles. Cut them out.

❷ On yellow construction paper, draw two ¼- by 4½-inch rectangles and two ¼- by 2½-inch rectangles. Cut them out.

❸ On red construction paper, draw two ¼- by 4-inch rectangles. Cut them out.

❹ On brown construction paper, draw two ¼- by 3½-inch rectangles. Cut them out.

❺ Take one of the rectangles and loop it over on itself without making a crease. Glue the ends of the loop together as shown. Repeat with the remaining rectangles. These are the tail feathers.

glue

**6** On brown construction paper, draw a 1- by 6-inch rectangle. Cut it out.

**7** Place the rectangle in front of you as shown. Draw a faint pencil line from one end of the strip to the other, ¼ inch from the top of the strip. Measure 3 inches from one end of the strip and make a faint pencil mark.

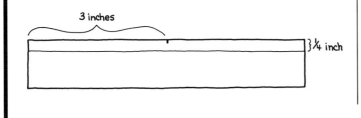

3 inches

¼ inch

**8** Take the two long orange feathers and glue them on either side of the pencil mark, with their bottom edges touching the pencil line. Glue the two long yellow feathers next to the orange feathers. Glue the two red feathers next to the yellow feathers. Glue the two brown feathers next to the red feathers. Glue the two short orange feathers next to the brown feathers. Glue the two short yellow feathers next to the orange feathers.

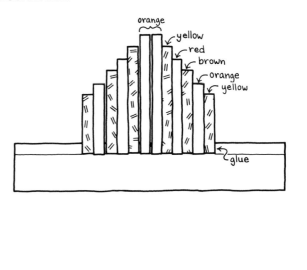

orange
yellow
red
brown
orange
yellow
glue

## THE HEAD:

**1** On brown construction paper, draw a ½- by 4½-inch rectangle. Cut it out.

**2** Curl one end of the rectangle around the end of your finger to form a loop. Glue the loop in place to make the head.

**3** Use construction paper and glue to give your turkey a face.

**4** Measure ½ inch from the uncurled end of the rectangle and make a light pencil mark. Fold on the pencil mark in the opposite direction from the loop, and crease it to form a tab.

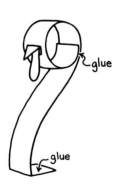

## TO ASSEMBLE:

**1** Measure 1 inch in from end of the toilet paper tube and mark with a pencil. Cut across the tube at the pencil mark to make a 1-inch ring. This is the turkey's body.

**2** Place the feathered strip in front of you with the side the feathers are glued to facing up. Apply a thin layer of glue to the strip. Wrap the strip around the toilet paper tube, overlapping the ends slightly. Hold until the glue is set.

3 Bend the feathers up to look like a turkey's tail.

4 Apply a thin layer of glue to the tab at the base of the turkey's neck and attach to the body. Hold in place until glue sets.

## Show Me the Way to Turkey, Texas

Where's the best place to celebrate Thanksgiving—except, of course, for Grandma's house? If you're hungry, you might try *Turkey, Texas*, or *Cranberry, Pennsylvania*, or *Pumpkin Center, California*. You can't beat *Mayflower, Arkansas*, or *Pilgrim Gardens, Pennsylvania*, for a traditional Thanksgiving. And *Blessing, Texas*, is the spot for people who want to remember the real reason we celebrate Thanksgiving.

# Set Sail on the Mayflower

**Tuna Boats Ahoy**

▼

**Storm-tossed Broccoli Salad**

▼

**Orange A-Float**

▼

**Seaworthy Raisin Rafts**

▼

*Shipshape Placemats*

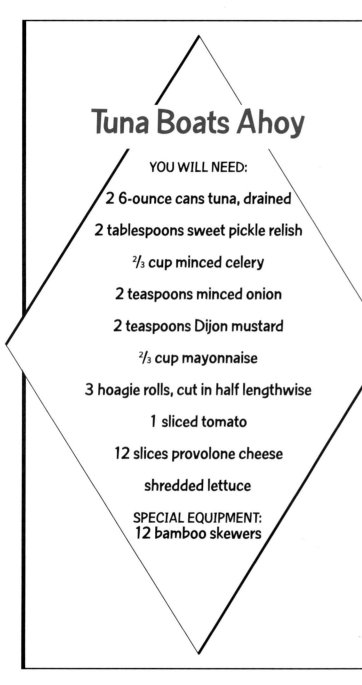

# Tuna Boats Ahoy

YOU WILL NEED:

2 6-ounce cans tuna, drained

2 tablespoons sweet pickle relish

$^2/_3$ cup minced celery

2 teaspoons minced onion

2 teaspoons Dijon mustard

$^2/_3$ cup mayonnaise

3 hoagie rolls, cut in half lengthwise

1 sliced tomato

12 slices provolone cheese

shredded lettuce

SPECIAL EQUIPMENT:
12 bamboo skewers

1 In a small bowl, combine tuna, relish, celery, onion, mustard, and mayonnaise. Stir well.

2 Use your fingers to scoop out a hollow on the inside of each of the six hoagie halves so they look like boats.

3 Divide the tuna mixture evenly among the boats. Top each sandwich with tomato slices.

4 Cut provolone cheese into squares and place on skewers to resemble masts.

5 Place two cheese "masts" in each boat.

6 Serve on a sea of lettuce.

Serves 6

# Storm-tossed Broccoli Salad

### YOU WILL NEED:

1 head broccoli, cut into bite-size pieces
(about 4 cups)

$^3/_4$ cup sliced black olives

$^1/_2$ red pepper, cleaned and chopped

3 carrots, peeled and thinly sliced

1 cup bottled Italian salad dressing

Parmesan cheese

1 In a large bowl, combine broccoli, olives, red pepper, and carrots.

2 Add dressing and toss.

3 Sprinkle with Parmesan cheese before serving.

**Serves 6**

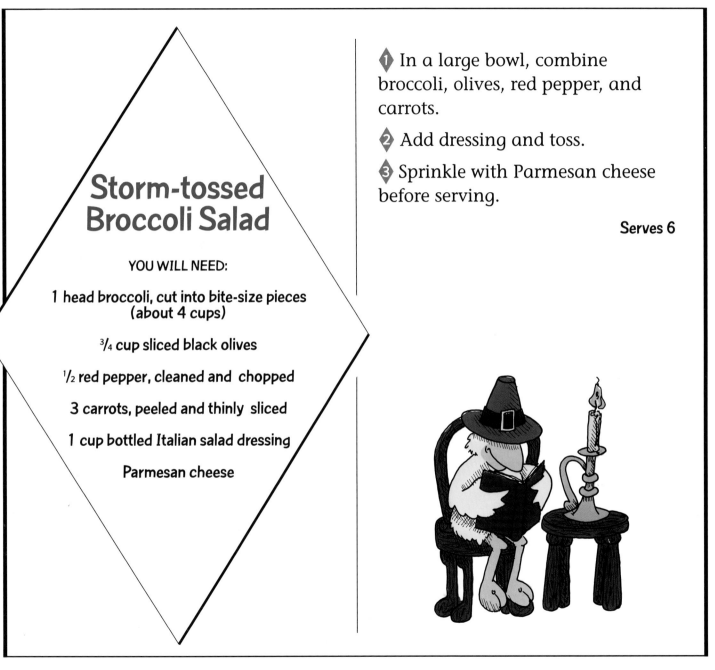

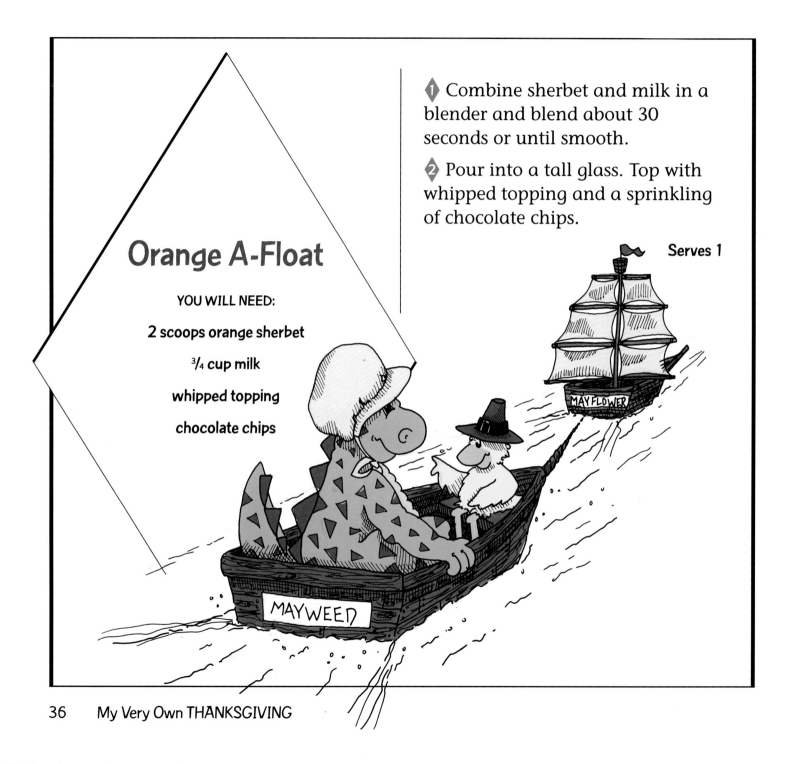

# Orange A-Float

**YOU WILL NEED:**

2 scoops orange sherbet

¾ cup milk

whipped topping

chocolate chips

1 Combine sherbet and milk in a blender and blend about 30 seconds or until smooth.

2 Pour into a tall glass. Top with whipped topping and a sprinkling of chocolate chips.

Serves 1

MAYFLOWER

MAYWEED

# Seaworthy Raisin Rafts

YOU WILL NEED:

3¼ cups graham cracker crumbs

1 cup raisins

2 cups unsweetened crispy rice cereal

1 14-ounce can sweetened condensed milk

1. Butter a 9- by 13-inch baking pan.

2. In a large bowl, combine graham cracker crumbs, raisins, and cereal and stir well.

3. Add milk and stir well. You can use your hands if you like.

4. Spread mixture evenly over bottom of pan and press into place with your hands or with the back of a spoon.

5. Let stand 15 minutes before cutting.

**Makes 20 bars**

# Shipshape Placemats

**YOU WILL NEED:**

tracing paper

pencil

scissors

1 medium potato

2 straight pins

paring knife

tempera paints

small brush

4 8- by 12-inch sheets of construction paper

◊ Place tracing paper over figures C and D on page 39 and trace around them. Cut out tracing paper patterns.

◊ Cut potato in half lengthwise. Pin the tracing paper boat to the smooth inside surface of one half of the potato and the mast to the other.

◊ Trace around the patterns with a sharp pencil, pushing the pencil point into the potato.

◊ Have an adult helper cut around the boat and mast shapes with a paring knife.

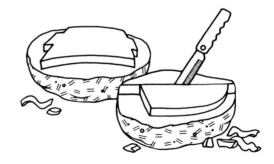

The excess potato should be trimmed away so each shape rises above the surface at least ½ inch.

⑤ Place a sheet of construction paper in front of you. Use a brush to apply paint to the raised boat shape on the potato. Press the painted side of the potato onto the paper. Print as many boats as you like, adding more paint when necessary.

⑥ Let the boat shapes dry. Then use the potato with the mast shape to print a mast on each boat.

⑦ Repeat steps 5 and 6 with the three remaining sheets of construction paper.

*Think of other shapes, such as stars and moons, to print with a potato.*

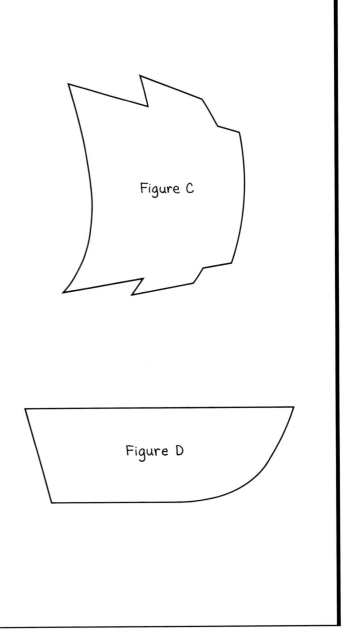

Figure C

Figure D

# The Big Game

**Halftime Ham Nibbles**
▼
**Potatoes Offside**
▼
**Festive Orange Salad**
▼
**Quarterback Caramel Pops**
▼
*It's a Party!*
*Invitations*

A PARTY!

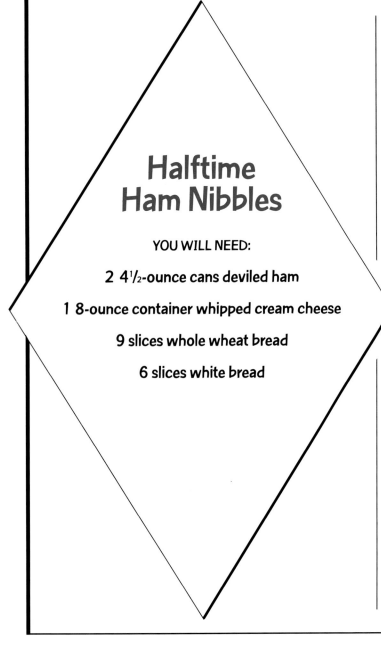

## Halftime Ham Nibbles

**YOU WILL NEED:**

2 4½-ounce cans deviled ham

1 8-ounce container whipped cream cheese

9 slices whole wheat bread

6 slices white bread

**1** In a small bowl, combine meat and cream cheese and stir well.

**2** Remove the crusts from the bread.

**3** Place three slices of wheat bread and two slices of white bread in front of you. Spread a slice of wheat bread with filling. Top with a slice of white bread and spread with filling. Repeat, alternating wheat and white bread. Top with a slice of wheat bread.

**4** Repeat step 3 two more times. You will have made three stacks.

**5** With a serrated knife, cut sandwich stacks into 1-inch-wide slices. Cut each slice in half.

**Serves 4 to 6**

# Potatoes Offside

YOU WILL NEED:

2 tablespoons olive oil

2 cloves garlic, peeled and minced

2 teaspoons crushed rosemary

4 large potatoes,
peeled and thinly sliced

1. Preheat oven to 375°.

2. Combine olive oil, garlic, and rosemary in a large bowl and stir well.

3. Add potatoes and toss to coat with olive oil mixture.

4. Spread potatoes evenly on a baking sheet.

5. Bake for 45 minutes or until golden brown.

**Serves 4 to 6**

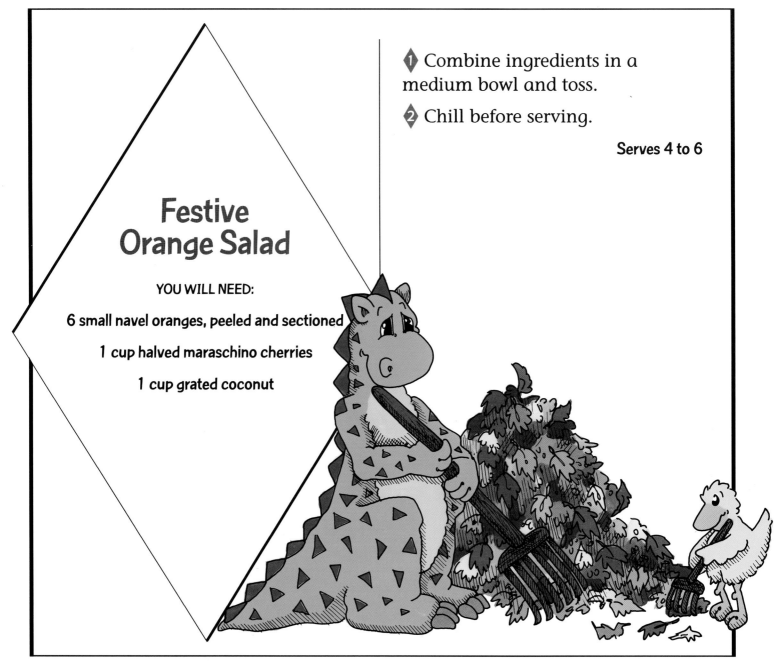

**1** Combine ingredients in a medium bowl and toss.

**2** Chill before serving.

Serves 4 to 6

# Festive Orange Salad

YOU WILL NEED:

6 small navel oranges, peeled and sectioned

1 cup halved maraschino cherries

1 cup grated coconut

# Quarterback Caramel Pops

**YOU WILL NEED:**

1 14-ounce package vanilla caramels
(about 50 pieces)

¼ cup milk

4 cups unsweetened crispy rice cereal

1 cup salted peanuts

**SPECIAL EQUIPMENT:**
9 popsicle sticks

**1** Grease an 8- by 8-inch pan.

**2** Combine caramels and milk in a large saucepan and cook over medium-low heat, stirring constantly, until caramels are melted. To microwave, combine caramels and milk in a large microwave-safe dish, and microwave on high 1 minute. Stir well. Microwave 1 more minute on high. Stir again. Repeat until caramels are melted.

**3** Add cereal and peanuts and stir well.

**4** Spread cereal mixture evenly in pan.

**5** Allow to set for 1 hour or until firm.

**6** Cut into 2-inch squares. Insert a popsicle stick in the middle of each square.

**Makes 9 pops**

# It's a Party! Invitations

**YOU WILL NEED:**

construction paper

leaf

pencil

scissors

decorating materials such as colored markers and glitter

**1** Fold a sheet of construction paper in half the short way.

**2** Place base of leaf on the fold and trace around the leaf.

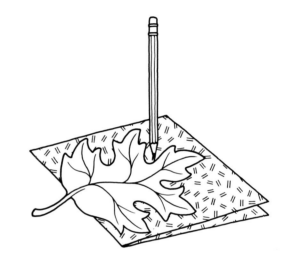

**3** Cut out the construction paper leaf. You will cut through two layers of construction paper.

**4** Repeat steps 1 through 3 to make as many invitations as you need.

⑤ Use materials such as colored markers and glitter to decorate your invitations. Be sure to write the date, time, and place of your party on the inside of the invitations.

*You can mail your invitations in large manila envelopes.*

## Going to Grandma's Game

You can play this game with as few as two people, but the more players there are, the more fun it will be. Arrange yourselves in a circle and choose someone to go first. That person begins by saying, "I'm going to Grandma's for Thanksgiving and I'm bringing . . ." The player then completes the sentence with a word that starts with the letter *A*. For instance, he or she might say ". . . and I'm bringing an apple." The next person must repeat what the first person said and then add an item that begins with the letter *B*. For instance, the second person might say, "I'm going to Grandma's for Thanksgiving and I'm bringing an apple and a blanket. Continue around the circle, always adding an item to the list that begins with the next letter of the alphabet. As the list grows longer, it will become harder to remember. If a player forgets any item on the list, he or she is out of the game. The last person left in the game is the winner.

# We Gather Together

Miles Standish Meat Loaf
▼
Pilgrim Peas
▼
Chocolate Cake to Share
▼
Tangy Lemon Ice Cream
▼

*Hand-in-Hand
Paper Dolls*

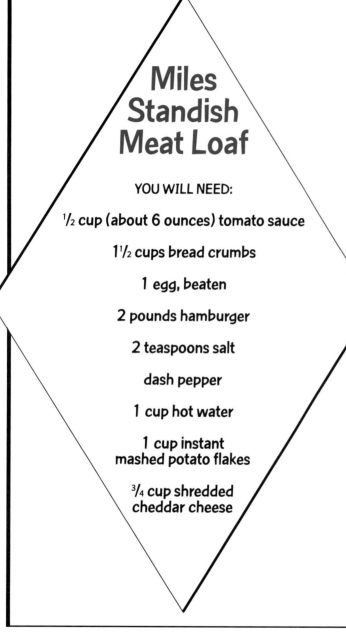

# Miles Standish Meat Loaf

**YOU WILL NEED:**

½ cup (about 6 ounces) tomato sauce

1½ cups bread crumbs

1 egg, beaten

2 pounds hamburger

2 teaspoons salt

dash pepper

1 cup hot water

1 cup instant mashed potato flakes

¾ cup shredded cheddar cheese

**1** Preheat oven to 350°.

**2** In a medium bowl, combine tomato sauce, bread crumbs, and beaten egg. Stir well.

**3** Add hamburger, salt, and pepper and mix well with hands.

**4** Spoon hamburger mixture into loaf pan. Smooth top with spoon.

**5** Cook for 1 hour.

**6** In a small bowl, combine hot water and instant potatoes. Stir well. Whip with a fork until fluffy.

**7** Frost meat loaf with potatoes. Cook for 15 minutes.

**8** Sprinkle with cheese and cook for 5 more minutes or until cheese is melted.

**Serves 6 to 8**

# Pilgrim Peas

1 tablespoon butter

1 cup sliced fresh mushrooms

2 10-ounce packages frozen peas

1 Melt butter in a small frying pan.

2 Add mushrooms and cook, stirring constantly, for about 5 minutes or until mushrooms are tender. Remove from heat.

3 Cook frozen peas according to package directions.

4 Add mushrooms to peas and toss.

**Serves 6 to 8**

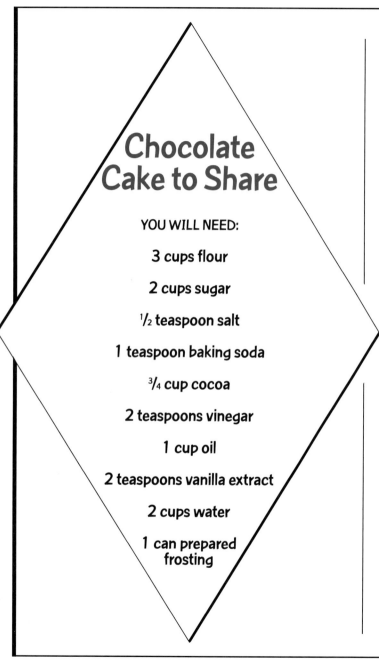

# Chocolate Cake to Share

**YOU WILL NEED:**

3 cups flour

2 cups sugar

$\frac{1}{2}$ teaspoon salt

1 teaspoon baking soda

$\frac{3}{4}$ cup cocoa

2 teaspoons vinegar

1 cup oil

2 teaspoons vanilla extract

2 cups water

1 can prepared frosting

1. Preheat oven to 350°.

2. Grease and flour a 9- by 13-inch baking pan.

3. In a large bowl, combine flour, sugar, salt, baking soda, and cocoa. Stir well.

4. Add vinegar, oil, vanilla, and water and beat with a spoon until smooth.

5. Pour batter into baking pan. Cook for 35 minutes or until toothpick poked into center of cake comes out clean.

6. When cake is cool, frost with prepared frosting.

**Makes 20 pieces**

# Tangy Lemon Ice Cream

**YOU WILL NEED:**

$1\frac{1}{2}$ **cups sugar**

**3 cups whipping cream**

$\frac{1}{3}$ **cup lemon juice**

$\frac{1}{4}$ **teaspoon salt**

1 Combine all ingredients in a large bowl and stir well.

2 Cover bowl and place in freezer.

3 Freeze overnight.

**Serves 6 to 8**

# A Thanksgiving Story

One of the most famous Thanksgiving tales is a love story. Captain Miles Standish was one of the leaders of Plymouth Colony, the settlement the Pilgrims founded in North America. It is said that Miles was a brave man and a strong leader, but there was one thing he just couldn't do. He didn't have the courage to ask a young Pilgrim woman named Priscilla Mullens to marry him. So Captain Standish asked his friend John Alden to propose for him.

John Alden didn't know what to do, for he was also in love with Priscilla. Because of his friendship with Miles, John went to Priscilla and told her about the captain's feelings. Priscilla listened to what John had to say and then, realizing John's true feelings, asked him to speak for himself.

When Captain Standish found out what had happened, he was very angry. But he finally realized what a good friend he had in John Alden, and he gave John and Priscilla his blessing.

This story is based on a poem by Henry Wadsworth Longfellow. No one knows how much of it really happened, but we do know that John and Priscilla married and had 11 children.

# Hand-in-Hand Paper Dolls

### YOU WILL NEED:

construction paper
(black, light brown, dark brown,
yellow, white, and red)

pencil

scissors

ruler

tracing paper

white liquid glue

8 inches of ⅛ -inch black ribbon

clear-drying glue
(look for Super Tacky
glue in sewing and
craft stores)

## PAPER DOLL FORM:

**1** On construction paper, draw a 4½- by 9-inch rectangle. (This will be the dolls' skin. Choose any color you want.) Cut it out.

**2** Place the rectangle in front of you as shown. Draw a faint pencil line from top to bottom, 3 inches from one side of the rectangle. Draw another faint pencil line from top to bottom, 3 inches from the other side of the rectangle. You will have divided the paper into three rectangles.

**3** Number the rectangles 1, 2, and 3 in the top right corner.

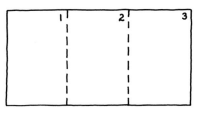

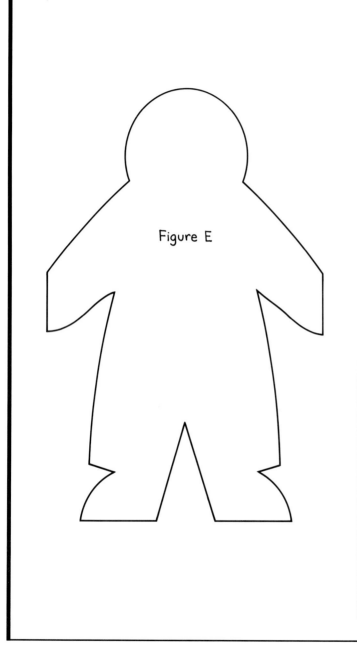

Figure E

4 Fold section 3 over the front of section 2. Turn paper over and fold section 1 over the back of section 2. You will end up with a 4½- by 3-inch rectangle, with section 1 on top.

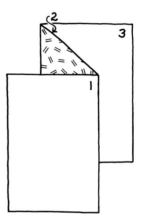

5 Place tracing paper over figure E at left and trace around it. Cut out tracing paper pattern.

6 Place pattern on section 1 of the folded rectangle and trace around it. Cut out paper dolls, cutting through all three layers of paper. Unfold the paper dolls. They will be connected at their hands.

## DRESSING THE PILGRIM MAN:

1 Place tracing paper over figures F-1 through F-10 on page 59 and trace. Cut out tracing paper patterns.

2 Place patterns for hat, jacket, and boots on black construction paper and trace around them. Cut out construction paper shapes.

3 Place patterns for hair, belt, and pants on dark brown construction paper and trace around them. Cut out construction paper shapes.

4 Place patterns for hat band and belt buckle on yellow construction paper and trace around them. Cut out construction paper shapes.

5 Place pattern for collar on white construction paper and trace around it. Cut out construction paper shape.

6 Glue the shapes to paper doll form with white liquid glue in the following order: boots, pants, jacket, belt, buckle, collar, hair, hat, hat band.

7 Cut a 4-inch piece of ribbon. Tie ribbon in a bow and attach to pilgrim man's collar with clear-drying glue.

## DRESSING THE NATIVE AMERICAN MAN:

1 Place tracing paper over figures G-1 through G-7 on page 60 and trace. Cut out tracing paper patterns.

2 Place patterns for collar, shirt, and pants/boots on dark brown construction paper and trace around them. Cut out construction paper shapes.

3 Place pattern for belt on light brown construction paper and trace around it. Cut out construction paper shape.

**4** Place pattern for hair on black construction paper and trace around it. Cut out construction paper shape.

**5** Place patterns for headband and feather on yellow construction paper and trace around them. Cut out construction paper shapes.

**6** Place pattern for feather on red construction paper and trace around it. Cut out construction paper shape.

**7** Glue the shapes to paper doll form with white liquid glue in the following order: pants/boots, shirt, collar, belt, hair, headband, feathers.

## DRESSING THE PILGRIM WOMAN:

**1** Place tracing paper over figures H-1 through H-8 on page 61 and trace. Cut out tracing paper patterns.

**2** Place patterns for dress and hat on black construction paper and trace around them. Cut out construction paper shapes.

**3** Place patterns for apron, collar, and hat brim on white construction paper and trace around them. Cut out construction paper shapes.

**4** Place patterns for hair and shoes on brown construction paper and trace around them. Cut out construction paper shapes.

**5** Glue the shapes to paper doll form with white liquid glue in the following order: shoes, dress, apron, collar, hair, hat, hat brim.

**6** Tie remaining 4 inches of ribbon in a bow and attach to pilgrim woman's collar with clear-drying glue.

# PILGRIM MAN

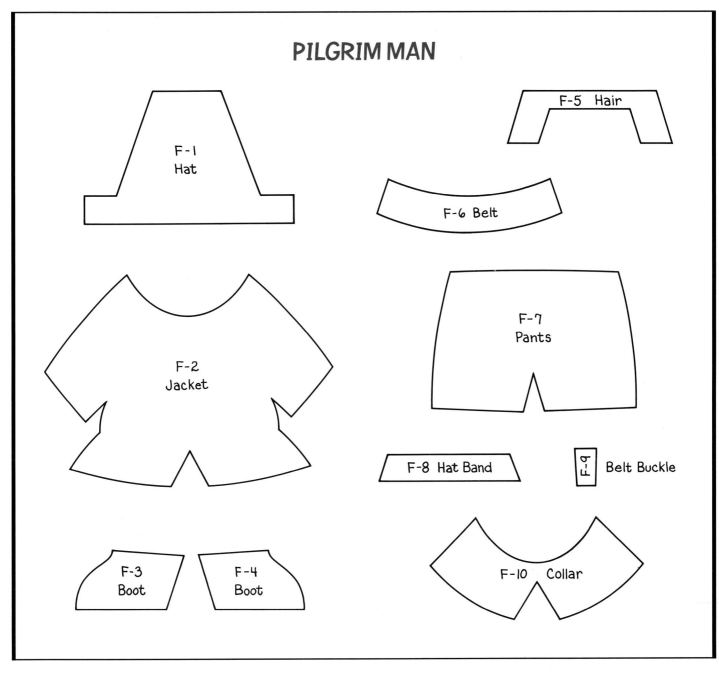

# NATIVE AMERICAN MAN

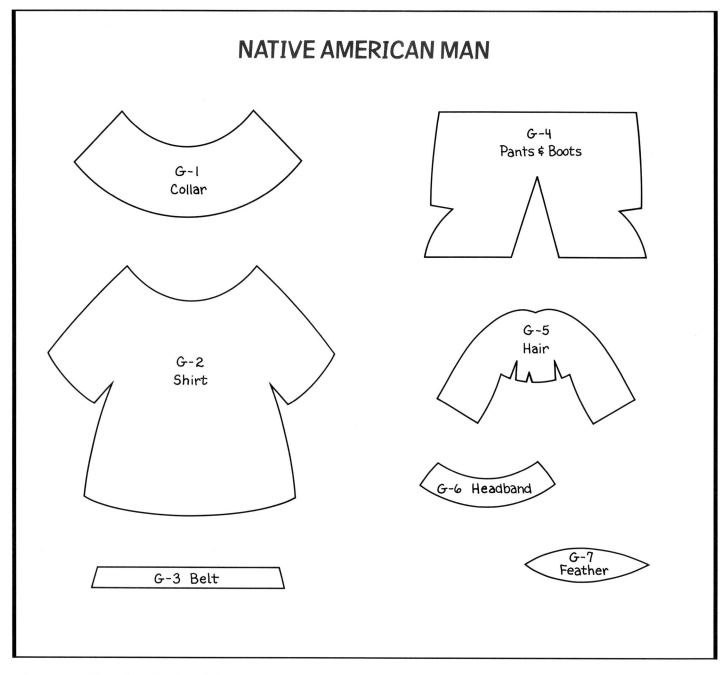

G-1
Collar

G-4
Pants & Boots

G-2
Shirt

G-5
Hair

G-6 Headband

G-7
Feather

G-3 Belt

My Very Own THANKSGIVING

# PILGRIM WOMAN

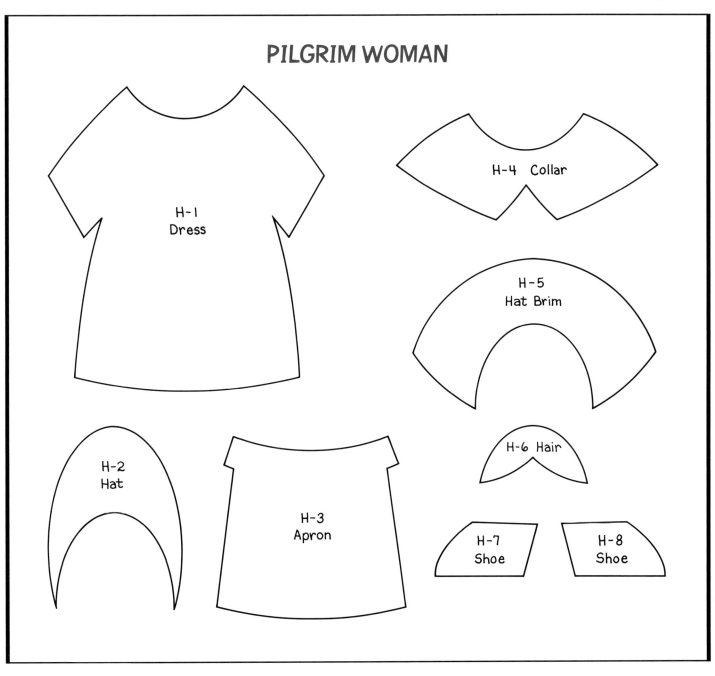

H-1 Dress

H-4 Collar

H-5 Hat Brim

H-6 Hair

H-2 Hat

H-3 Apron

H-7 Shoe

H-8 Shoe

# Recipe List

## Beverages
Sparkling Cider
Orange A-Float

## Side Dishes
Squanto's Squash
Basket o' Biscuits
Eat Your Veggies Pizza
Storm-Tossed Broccoli Salad
Potatoes Offside
Festive Orange Salad
Pilgrim Peas

## Main Dishes
Heapin' Helpin' Chicken
Savory Cheese Soup
Tuna Boats Ahoy
Halftime Ham Nibbles
Miles Standish Meat Loaf

## Desserts
Chilly Chocolate Pumpkin Pie
Just Peachy
Seaworthy Raisin Rafts
Quarterback Caramel Pops
Chocolate Cake to Share
Tangy Lemon Ice Cream

# Glossary

**bamboo skewer**—a slender, pointed stick used to hold food in place

**colander**—a bowl-shaped container with holes in the bottom for draining the liquid from a food

**cornstarch**—a white powder made from corn that is used to thicken liquids

**crease**—run your fingers firmly along a fold so that the fold mark remains

**deviled ham**—a mixture of finely chopped ham and seasonings

**Dijon mustard**—a dark, strong-flavored mustard

**drain**—pour the liquid off of a food

**drizzle**—pour a thin stream of liquid over a food in a random pattern

**fold**—mix by scooping up a substance with a spoon and turning it over on itself

**grate**—tear a food into small pieces by rubbing it against a grater

**grease**—coat with a thin layer of butter, margarine, or shortening

**hoagie roll**—a long, submarine-shaped roll

**maraschino cherries**—bright red cherries in a sweet syrup

**mince**—cut into very small pieces

**navel orange**—a seedless orange with a round hollow resembling a navel on one end

**olive oil**—a clear, golden oil made from olives

**preheat**—allow an oven to heat up to a certain temperature

**provolone cheese**—a firm, cream-colored cheese

**shred**—cut into long, ragged pieces

**sparkling water**—water with carbonation added

**sweetened condensed milk**—milk with some of the water removed and sugar added

**sweet pickle relish**—chopped up sweet pickles

**tempera paint**—a thick, fast-drying paint, often called poster paint

**toss**—combine foods by lightly lifting, turning, and dropping with a fork

**trace**—copy a pattern onto another piece of paper

**tracing paper**—paper thin enough to be seen through when placed on top of a pattern

**transparent**—clear enough to see through

**vanilla extract**—a liquid used to give a vanilla flavor to foods

# Index